MW01201408

let's play
I SPY...
christmas

Copyright @2019 by **Kiddie Coloring Books**
All rights reserved.

For any inquiries or questions regarding our books,
please contact us at : **kiddiecoloringbooks@gmail.com**

ISBN: 9781701090064

(Image by Freepik)

are you ready to play i spy ?

the letters are not in alphabetical order, just like a real game of i spy.

i spy with my little eye, something beginning with...

A

A is for...

Angel

i spy with my little eye, something beginning with...

U

U is for...
Unicorn

i spy with my little eye, something beginning with...

C

C is for...
Candle

i spy with my little eye, something beginning with...

L

L is for...

Lamp

i spy with my little eye, something beginning with...

M

M is for...
Mitten

i spy with my little eye, something beginning with...

B

B is for...

Bell

i spy with my little eye, something beginning with...

G is for...
Gift

i spy with my little eye, something beginning with...

P

P is for...
Penguin

i spy with my little eye, something beginning with...

K

K is for...
King

i spy with my little eye, something beginning with...

M

M is for...
Mouse

i spy with my little eye, something beginning with...

N

N is for...
Nutcracker

i spy with my little eye, something beginning with...

S

S is for...
Santa Claus

i spy with my little eye, something beginning with...

R

R is for...

Reindeer

i spy with my little eye, something beginning with...

C

C is for...
Cookie

i spy with my little eye, something beginning with...

G

G is for...

Gingerbread

i spy with my little eye, something beginning with...

S

S is for...
Snowman

i spy with my little eye, something beginning with...

C

C is for...
Cat

i spy with my little eye, something beginning with...

B

B is for...
Bear

i spy with my little eye, something beginning with...

D

D is for...

Dog

Merry Christmas

Made in the USA
Columbia, SC
24 November 2019

83766139R00024